The Great Passion

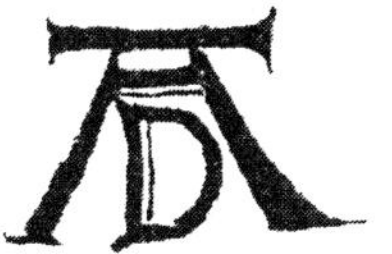

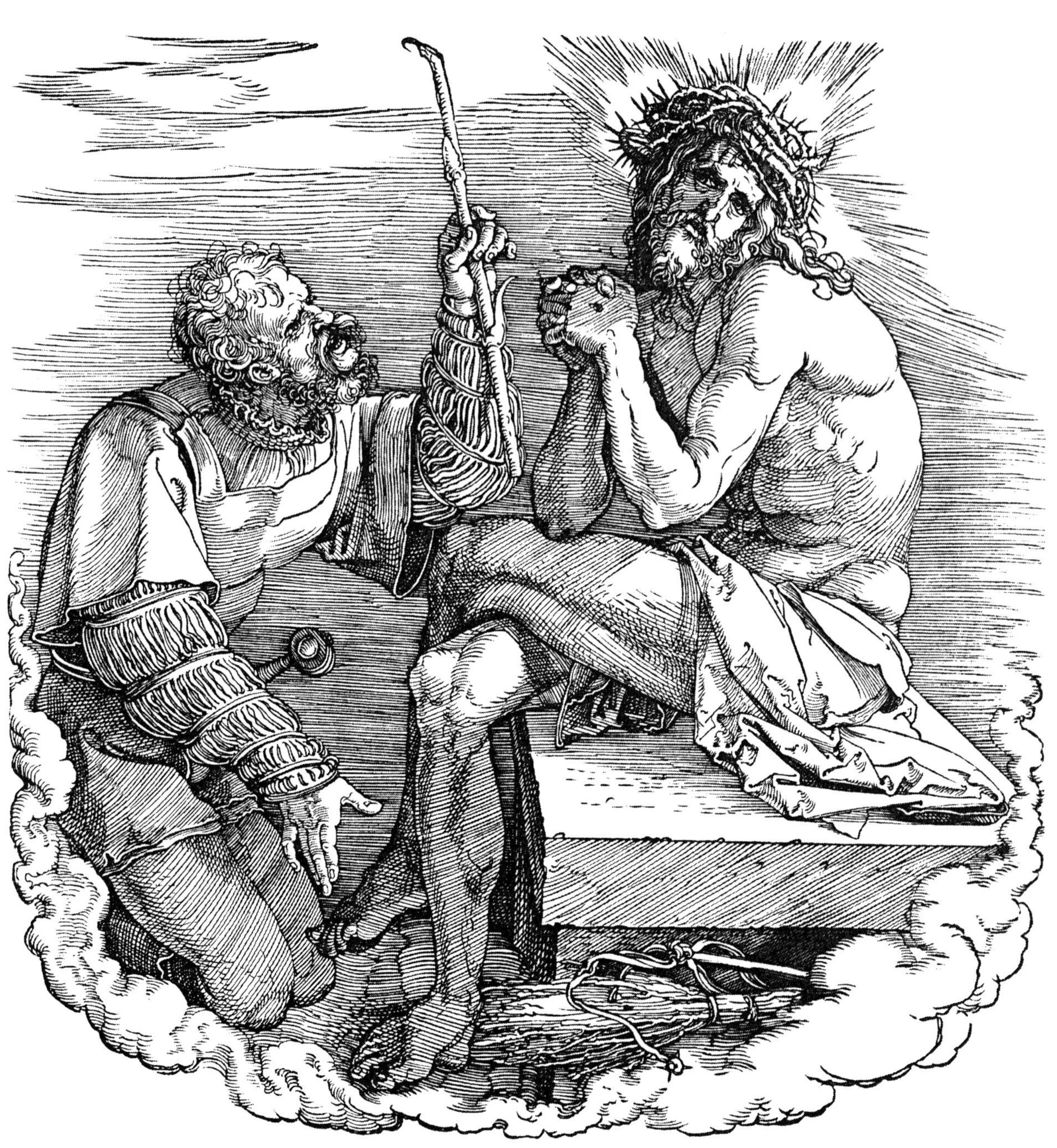

THE GREAT PASSION

Albrecht
Dürer

PALLAS 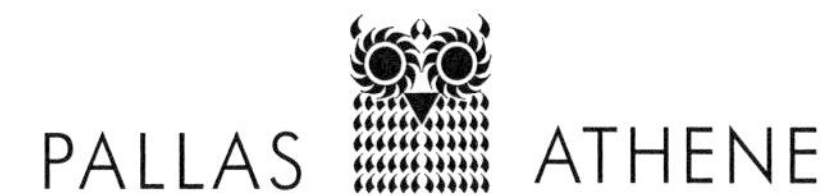 ATHENE

I. THE LAST SUPPER

21 When Jesus had thus said, he was troubled in spirit, and testified, and said,
Verily, verily, I say unto you, that one of you shall betray me.
22 Then the disciples looked one on another, doubting of whom he spake.
23 Now there was leaning on Jesus' bosom one of his disciples,
whom Jesus loved.
24 Simon Peter therefore beckoned to him, that he should ask
who it should be of whom he spake.
25 He then lying on Jesus' breast saith unto him, Lord, who is it?
26 Jesus answered, He it is, to whom I shall give a sop, when I have dipped it.
And when he had dipped the sop, he gave it to Judas Iscariot,
the son of Simon.
27 And after the sop Satan entered into him. Then said Jesus unto him,
That thou doest, do quickly.
28 Now no man at the table knew for what intent he spake this unto him.
29 For some of them thought, because Judas had the bag, that Jesus had
said unto him, Buy those things that we have need of against the feast;
or, that he should give something to the poor.
30 He then having received the sop went immediately out:
and it was night.
31 Therefore, when he was gone out, Jesus said,
Now is the Son of man glorified, and God is glorified in him.
32 If God be glorified in him, God shall also glorify him in himself,
and shall straightway glorify him.

JOHN, CHAPTER 13, VERSES 21-32

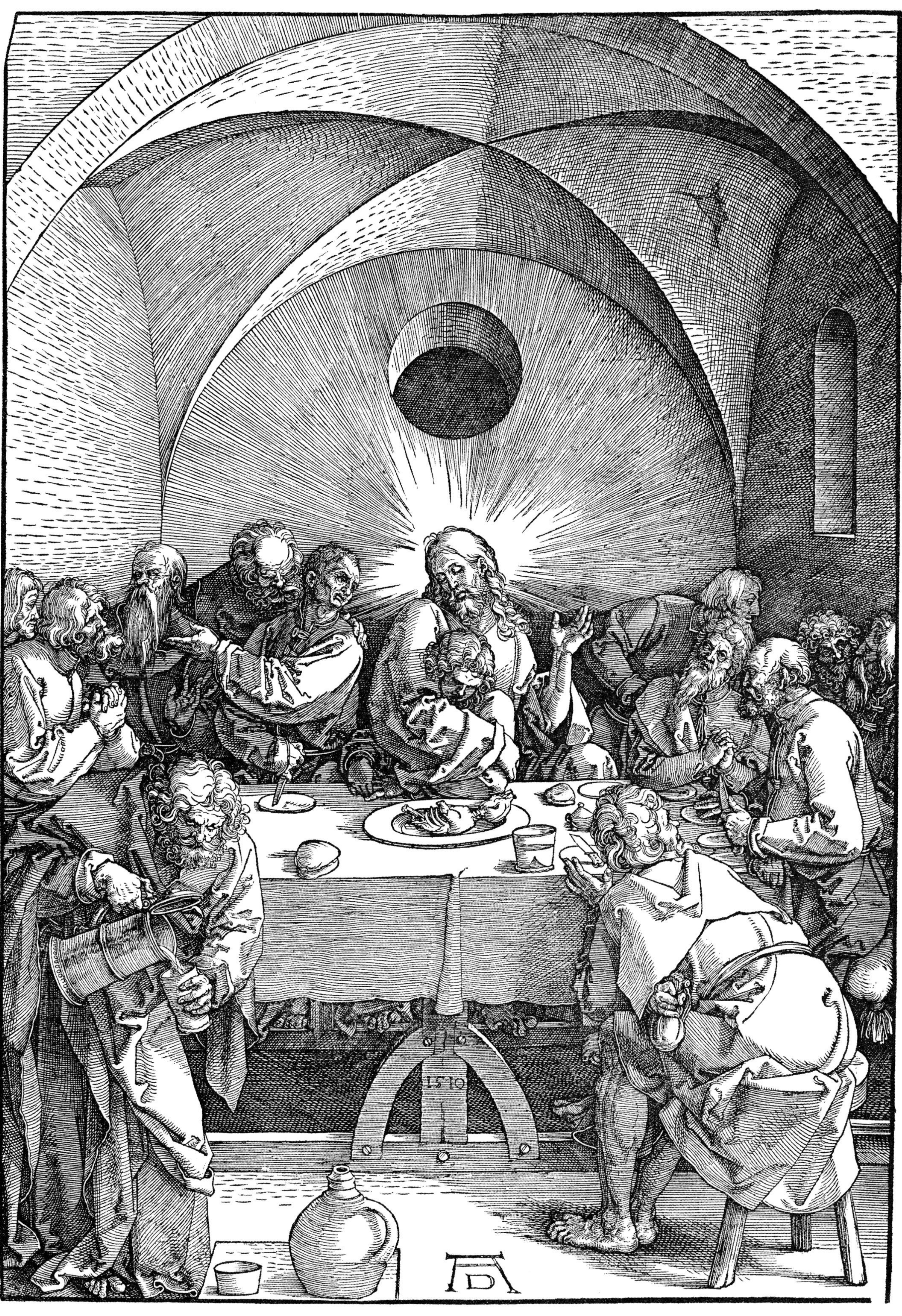
1510

2. THE AGONY IN THE GARDEN

39 And he came out, and went, as he was wont, to the mount of Olives;
and his disciples also followed him.
40 And when he was at the place, he said unto them,
Pray that ye enter not into temptation.
41 And he was withdrawn from them about a stone's cast,
and kneeled down, and prayed,
42 Saying, Father, if thou be willing, remove this cup from me:
nevertheless not my will, but thine, be done.
43 And there appeared an angel unto him from heaven, strengthening him.
44 And being in an agony he prayed more earnestly: and his sweat was
as it were great drops of blood falling down to the ground.
45 And when he rose up from prayer, and was come to his disciples,
he found them sleeping for sorrow,
46 And said unto them, Why sleep ye? rise and pray,
lest ye enter into temptation.
47 And while he yet spake, behold a multitude, and he that was called Judas,
one of the twelve, went before them, and drew near unto Jesus to kiss him.

LUKE, CHAPTER 22, VERSES 39-47

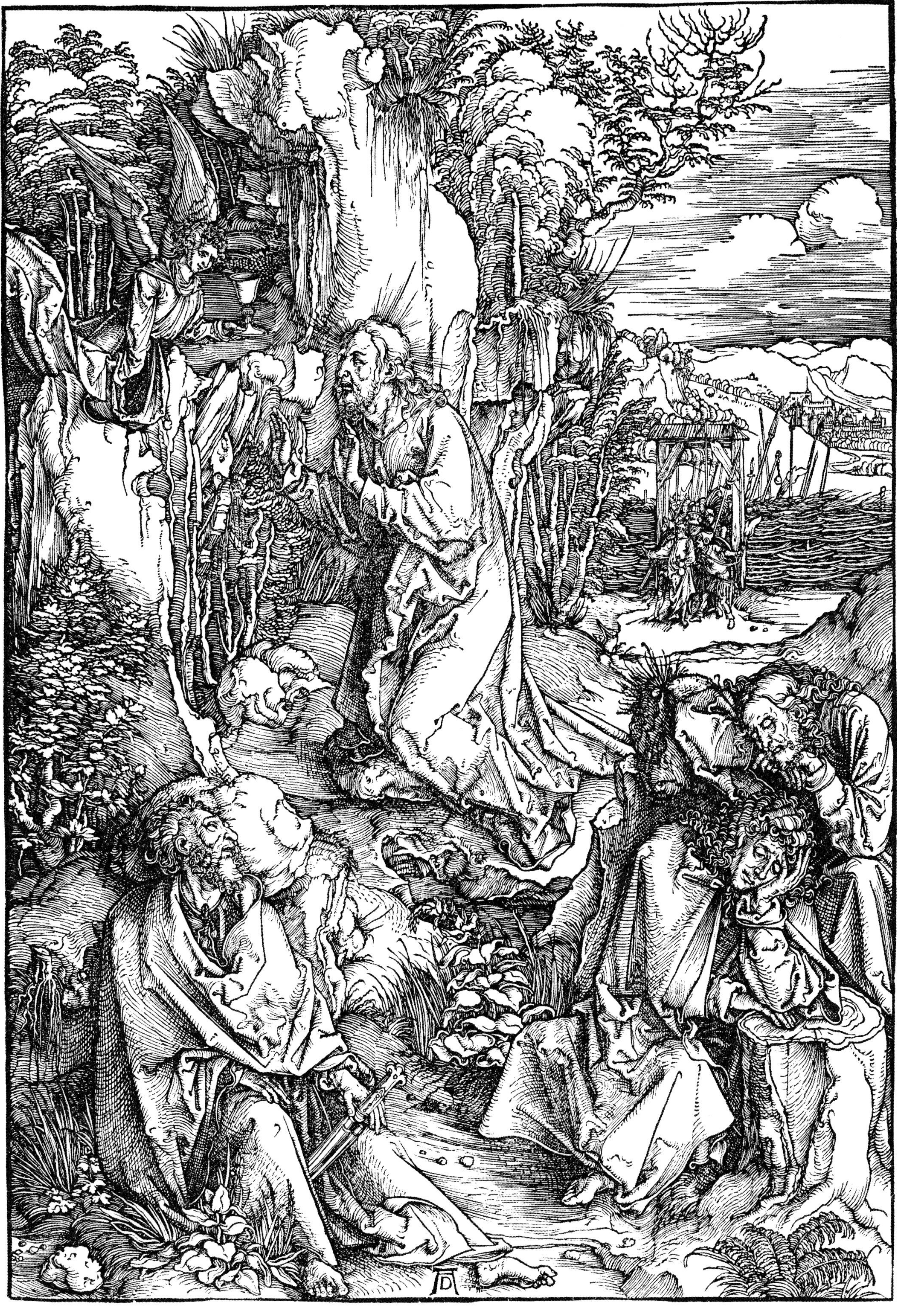

3. THE ARREST

43 And immediately, while he yet spake, cometh Judas, one of the twelve,
and with him a great multitude with swords and staves,
from the chief priests and the scribes and the elders.
44 And he that betrayed him had given them a token, saying,
Whomsoever I shall kiss, that same is he; take him,
and lead him away safely.
45 And as soon as he was come, he goeth straightway to him,
and saith, Master, master; and kissed him.
46 And they laid their hands on him, and took him.
47 And one of them that stood by drew a sword, and smote a servant
of the high priest, and cut off his ear.
48 And Jesus answered and said unto them, Are ye come out,
as against a thief, with swords and with staves to take me?
49 I was daily with you in the temple teaching, and ye took me not:
but the scriptures must be fulfilled.
50 And they all forsook him, and fled.
51 And there followed him a certain young man, having a linen cloth
cast about his naked body; and the young men laid hold on him:
52 and he left the linen cloth, and fled from them naked.

MARK, CHAPTER 14, VERSES 43-52

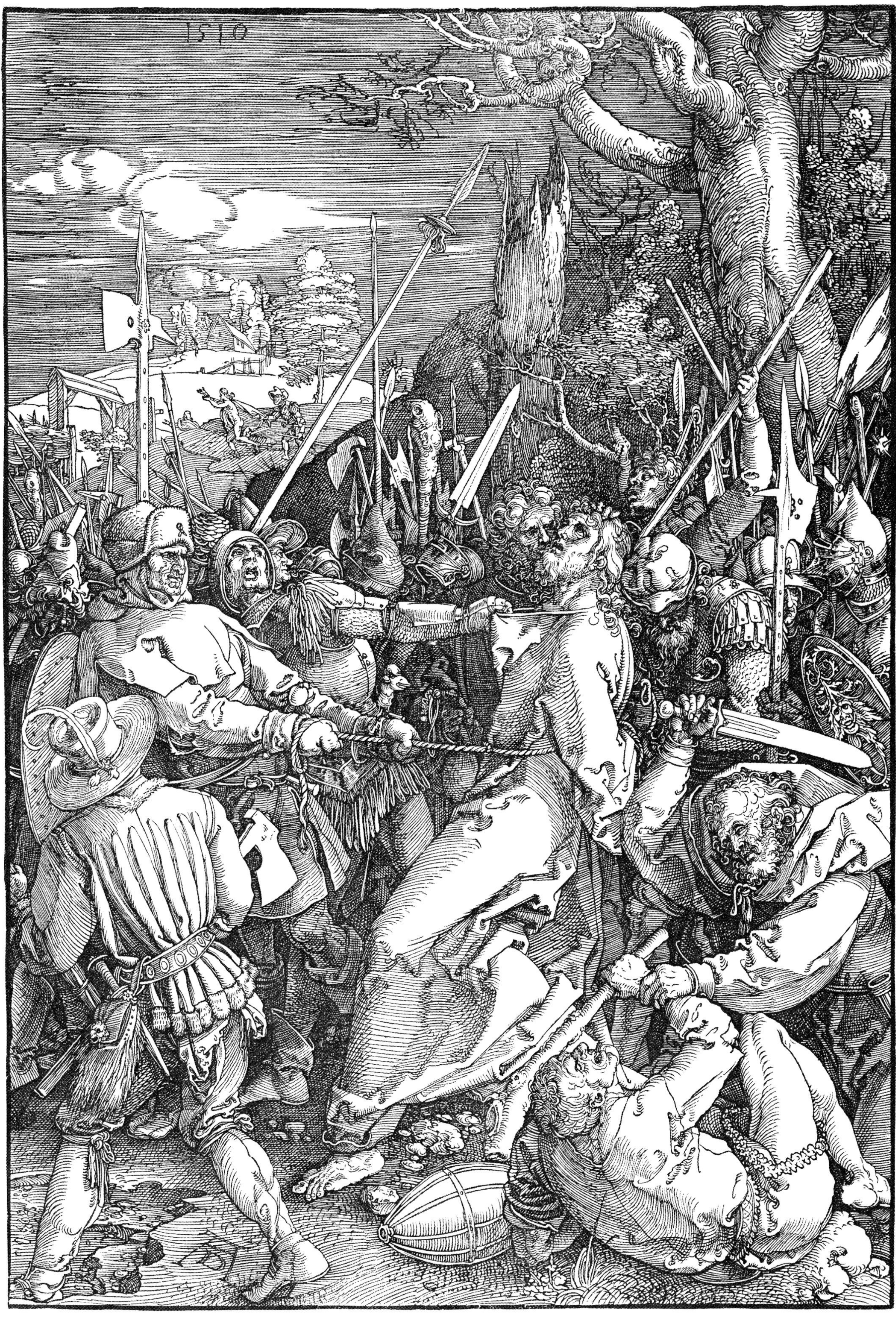
1510

4. THE FLAGELLATION

1 Then Pilate therefore took Jesus, and scourged him.

JOHN, CHAPTER 19, VERSE 1

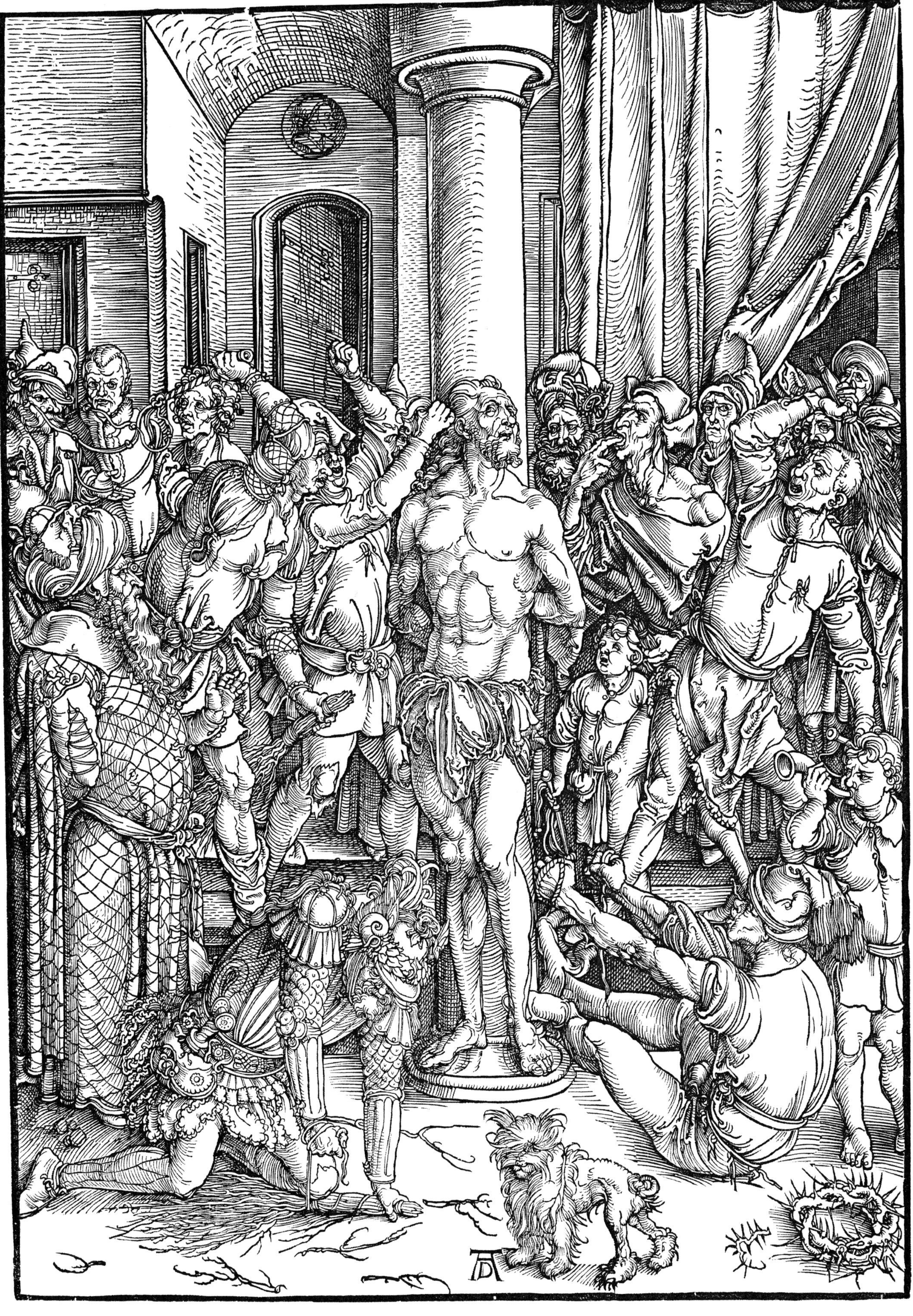

5. ECCE HOMO

4 Pilate therefore went forth again, and saith unto them,
Behold, I bring him forth to you, that ye may know that I find no fault in him.
5 Then came Jesus forth, wearing the crown of thorns, and the purple robe.
And Pilate saith unto them, Behold the man!
6 When the chief priests therefore and officers saw him, they cried out, saying,
Crucify him, crucify him. Pilate saith unto them,
Take ye him, and crucify him: for I find no fault in him.
7 The Jews answered him, We have a law, and by our law he ought to die,
because he made himself the Son of God.

JOHN, CHAPTER 19, VERSES 4-7

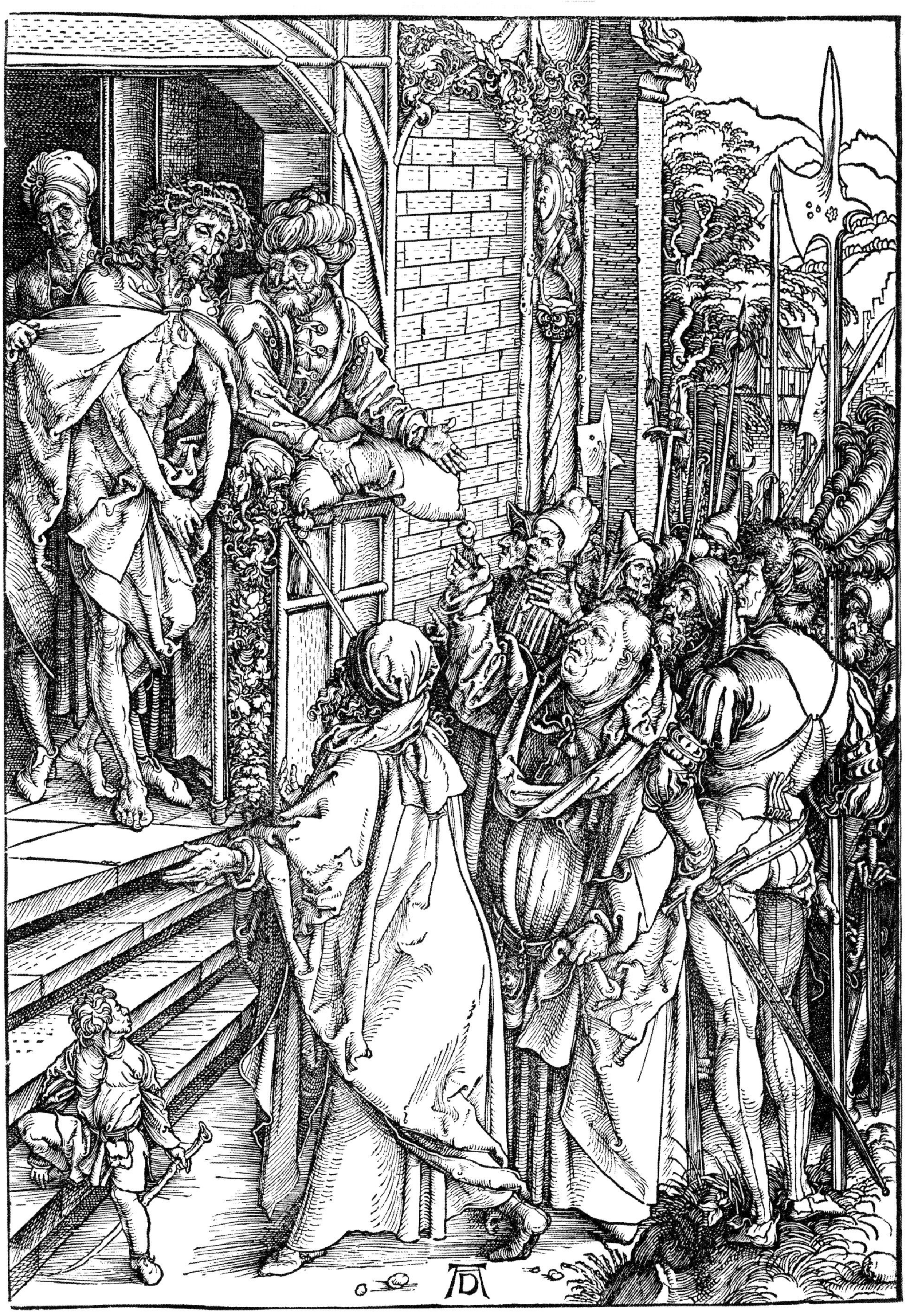

6. THE WAY OF THE CROSS

26 And as they led him away, they laid hold upon one Simon, a Cyrenian,
coming out of the country, and on him they laid the cross,
that he might bear it after Jesus.
27 And there followed him a great company of people, and of women,
which also bewailed and lamented him.
28 But Jesus turning unto them said, Daughters of Jerusalem, weep not for me,
but weep for yourselves, and for your children.
29 For, behold, the days are coming, in the which they shall say,
Blessed are the barren, and the wombs that never bare,
and the paps which never gave suck.
30 Then shall they begin to say to the mountains, Fall on us;
and to the hills, Cover us.
31 For if they do these things in a green tree, what shall be done in the dry?

LUKE, CHAPTER 23, VERSES 26-31

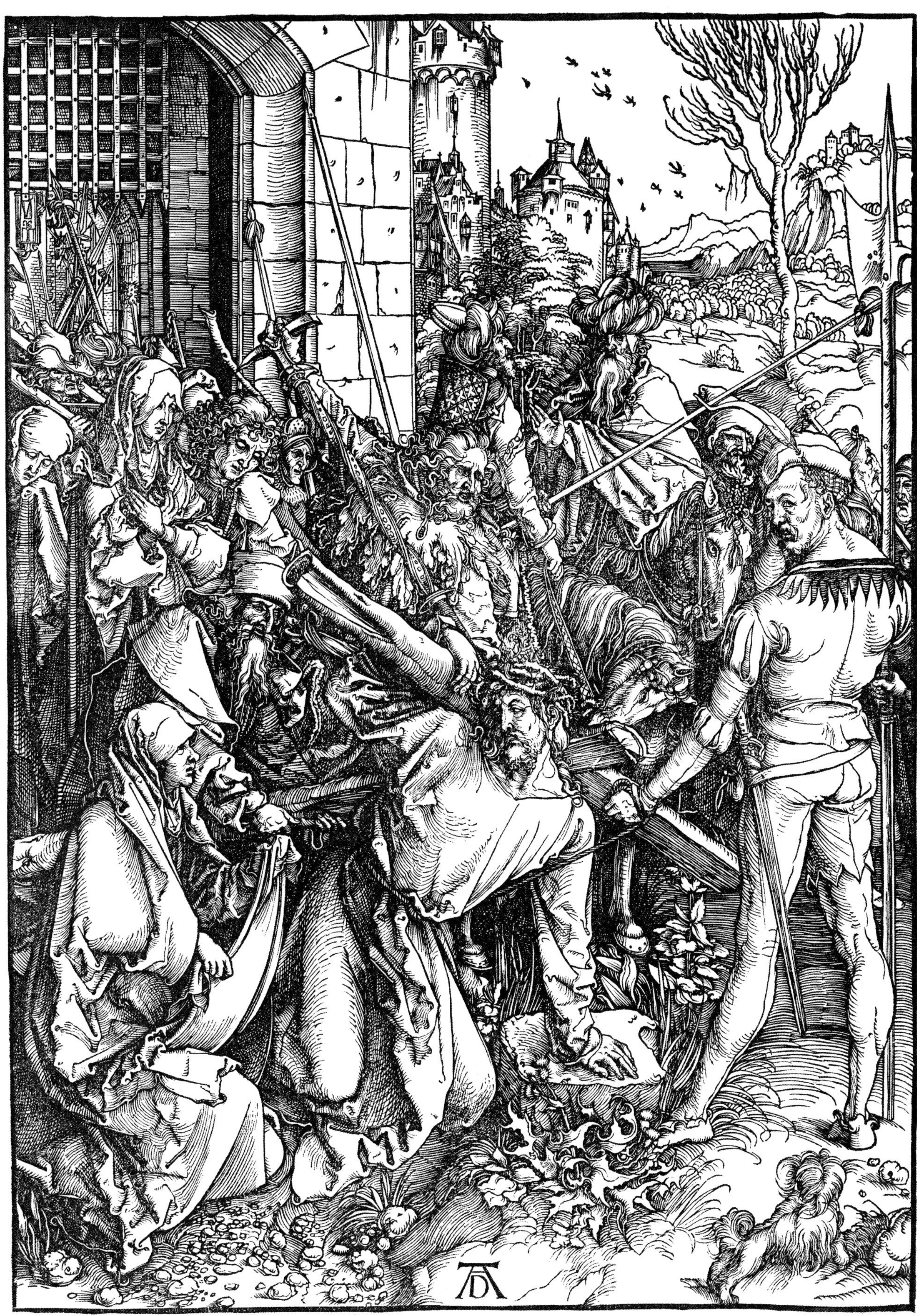

7. THE CRUCIFIXION

22 And they bring him unto the place Golgotha,
which is, being interpreted, The place of a skull.
26 And the superscription of his accusation was written over,
THE KING OF THE JEWS.

MARK, CHAPTER 15, VERSES 22 AND 26

25 Now there stood by the cross of Jesus his mother, and his mother's sister,
Mary the wife of Cleophas, and Mary Magdalene.
26 When Jesus therefore saw his mother, and the disciple standing by,
whom he loved, he saith unto his mother, Woman, behold thy son!
27 Then saith he to the disciple, Behold thy mother!
And from that hour that disciple took her unto his own home.

JOHN, CHAPTER 19, VERSES 25-27

44 And it was about the sixth hour, and there was a darkness
over all the earth until the ninth hour.
45 And the sun was darkened, and the veil of the temple was rent in the midst.
46 And when Jesus had cried with a loud voice, he said,
Father, into thy hands I commend my spirit:
and having said thus, he gave up the ghost.
47 Now when the centurion saw what was done, he glorified God, saying,
Certainly this was a righteous man.

LUKE, CHAPTER 23, VERSES 44-47

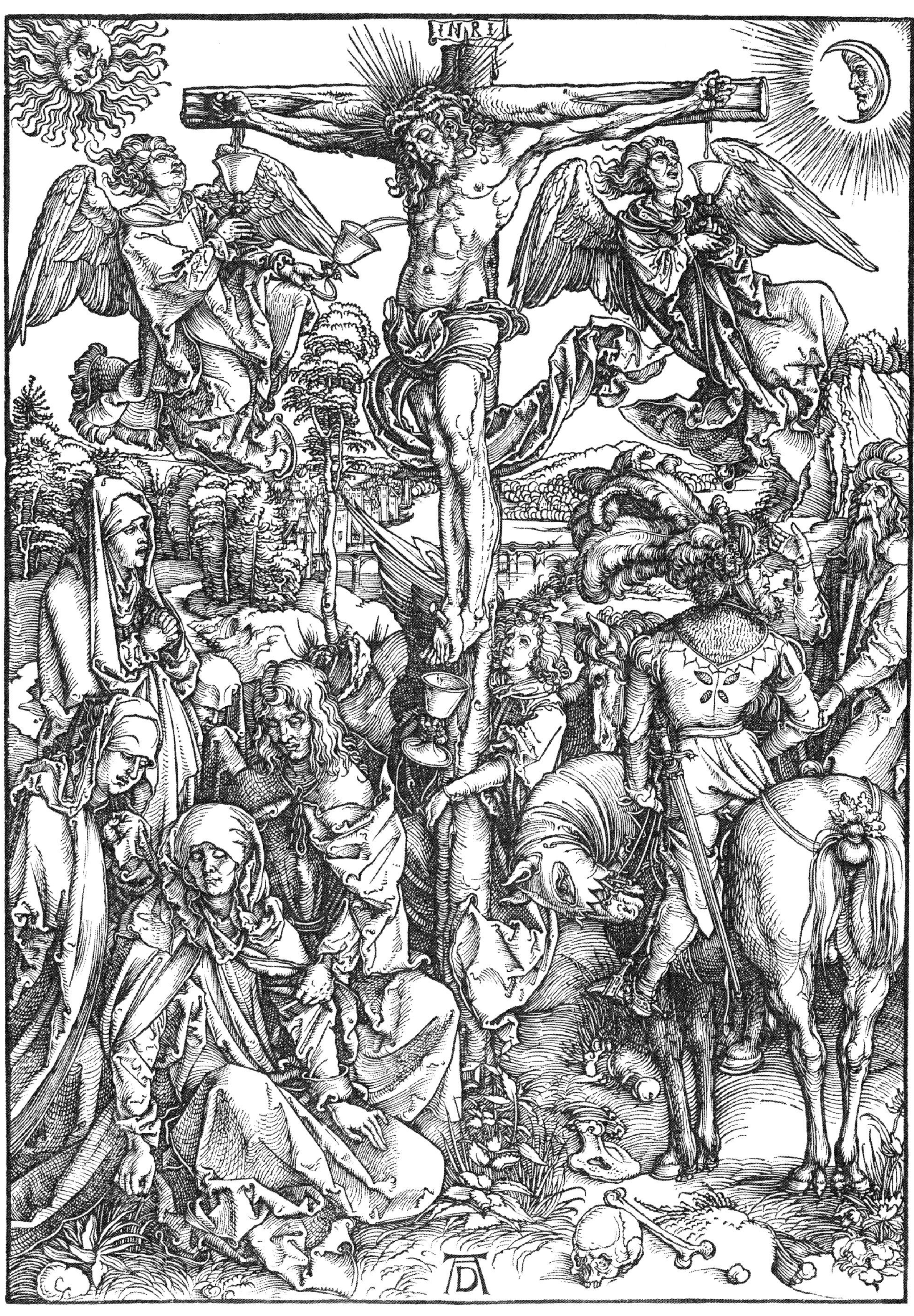
INRI

8. THE LAMENTATION

55 And many women were there beholding afar off, which followed
Jesus from Galilee, ministering unto him:
56 among which was Mary Magdalene, and Mary the mother of
James and Joses, and the mother of Zebedee's children.

MATTHEW, CHAPTER 27, VERSES 55-56

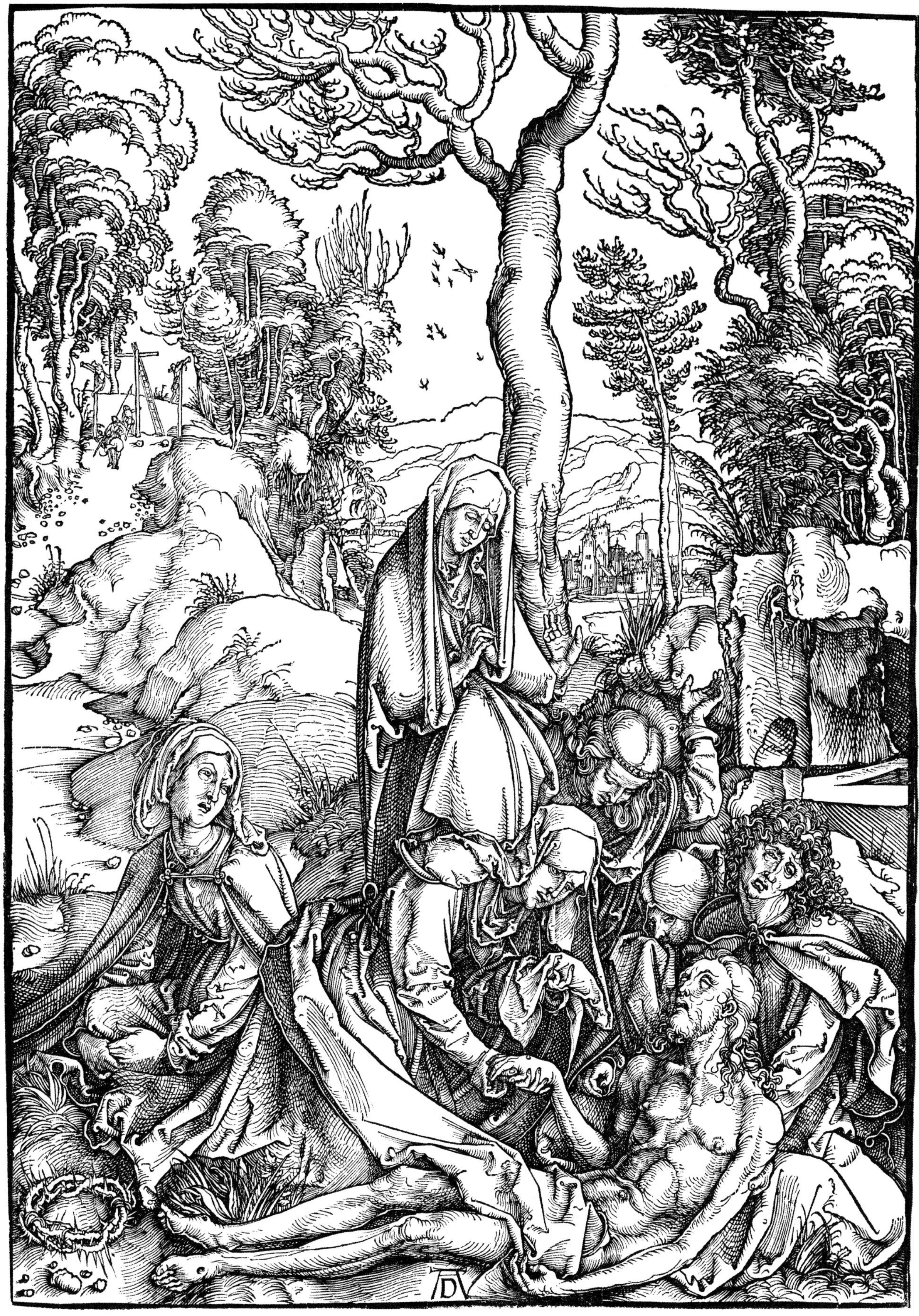

9. THE ENTOMBMENT

57 When the even was come, there came a rich man of Arimathæa,
named Joseph, who also himself was Jesus' disciple:
58 he went to Pilate, and begged the body of Jesus. Then Pilate
commanded the body to be delivered.
59 And when Joseph had taken the body, he wrapped it in a clean linen cloth,
60 and laid it in his own new tomb, which he had hewn out in the rock:
and he rolled a great stone to the door of the sepulchre, and departed.
61 And there was Mary Magdalene, and the other Mary,
sitting over against the sepulchre.

MATTHEW, CHAPTER 27, VERSES 57-61

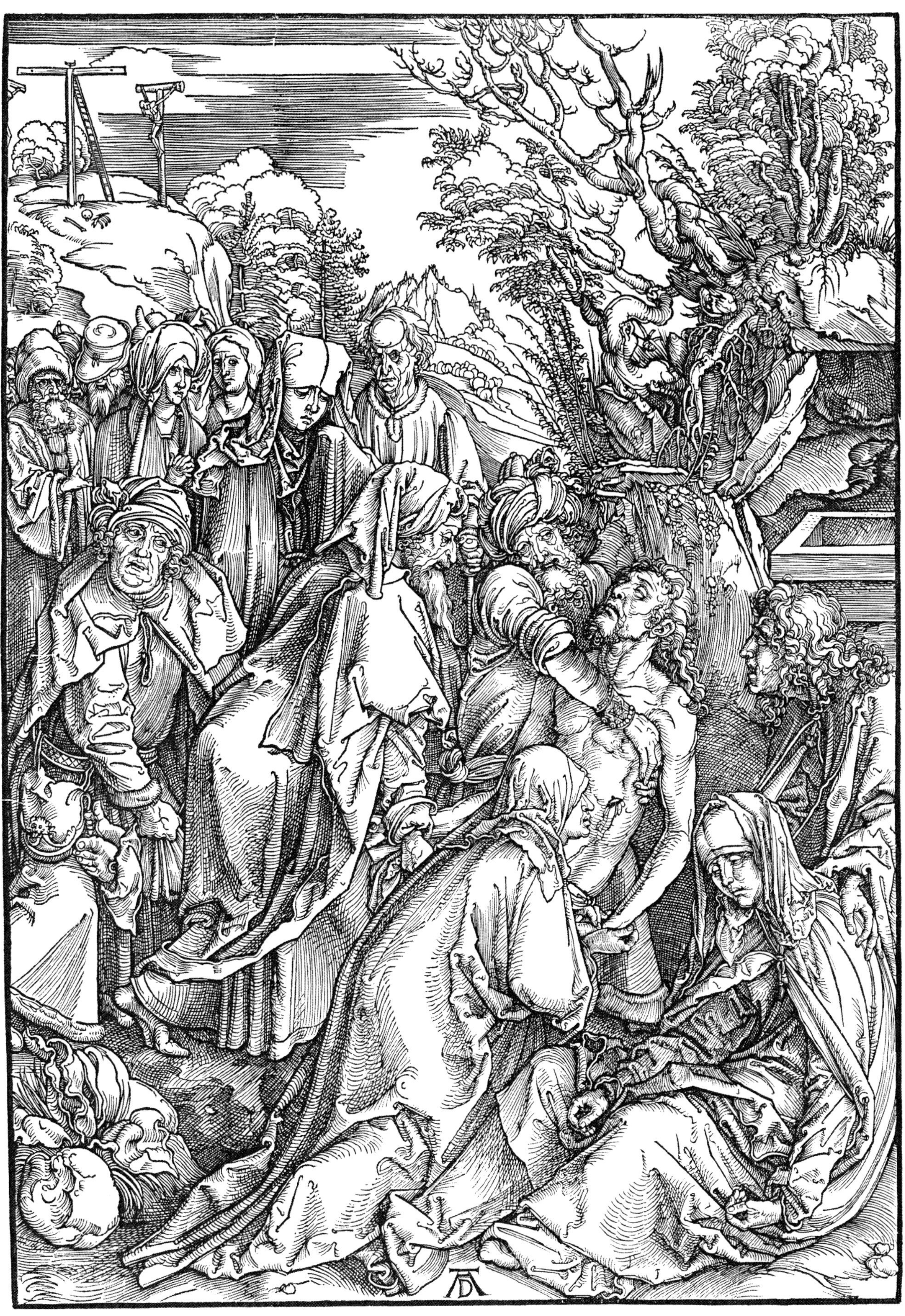

10. CHRIST DESCENDS INTO LIMBO

2 And Christ himself on a sudden appearing in their habitations;
they cried out therefore, and said, We are bound by thee;
thou seemest to intend our confusion before the Lord.
3 Who art thou, who hast no sign of corruption, but that bright appearance which
is a full proof of thy greatness, of which yet thou seemest to take no notice?
4 Who art thou, so powerful and so weak, so great and so little, a mean and
yet a soldier of the first rank, who can command in the form of
a servant as a common soldier?
5 The King of Glory, dead and alive, though once slain upon the cross?
6 Who layest dead in the grave, and art come down alive to us, and in thy death
all the creatures trembled, and all the stars were moved, and now hast thou
thy liberty among the dead, and givest disturbance to our legions?
7 Who art thou, who dost release the captives that were held in chains
by original sin, and bringest them into their former liberty
8 Who art thou, who dost spread so glorious and divine a light over
those who were made blind by the darkness of sin?
9 In like manner all the legions of devils were seized with the like horror,
and with the most submissive fear cried out, and said,
10 Whence comes it, O thou Jesus Christ, that thou art a man so powerful and
glorious in majesty, so bright as to have no spot, and so pure as to have no crime?
For that lower world of earth, which was ever till now subject to us, and from
whence we received tribute, never sent us such a dead man before,
never sent such presents as these to the princes of hell.
11 Who therefore art thou, who with such courage enterest among our abodes,
and art not only not afraid to threaten us with the greatest punishments, but
also endeavourest to rescue all others from the chains in which we hold them?
12 Perhaps thou art that Jesus, of whom Satan just now spoke to our prince,
that by the death of the cross thou wert about to receive the power of death.
13 Then the King of Glory trampling upon death, seized the prince of hell,
deprived him of all his power, and took our earthly father Adam
with him to his glory.

APOCRYPHAL GOSPEL OF NICODEMUS, CHAPTER 17, VERSES 2-13

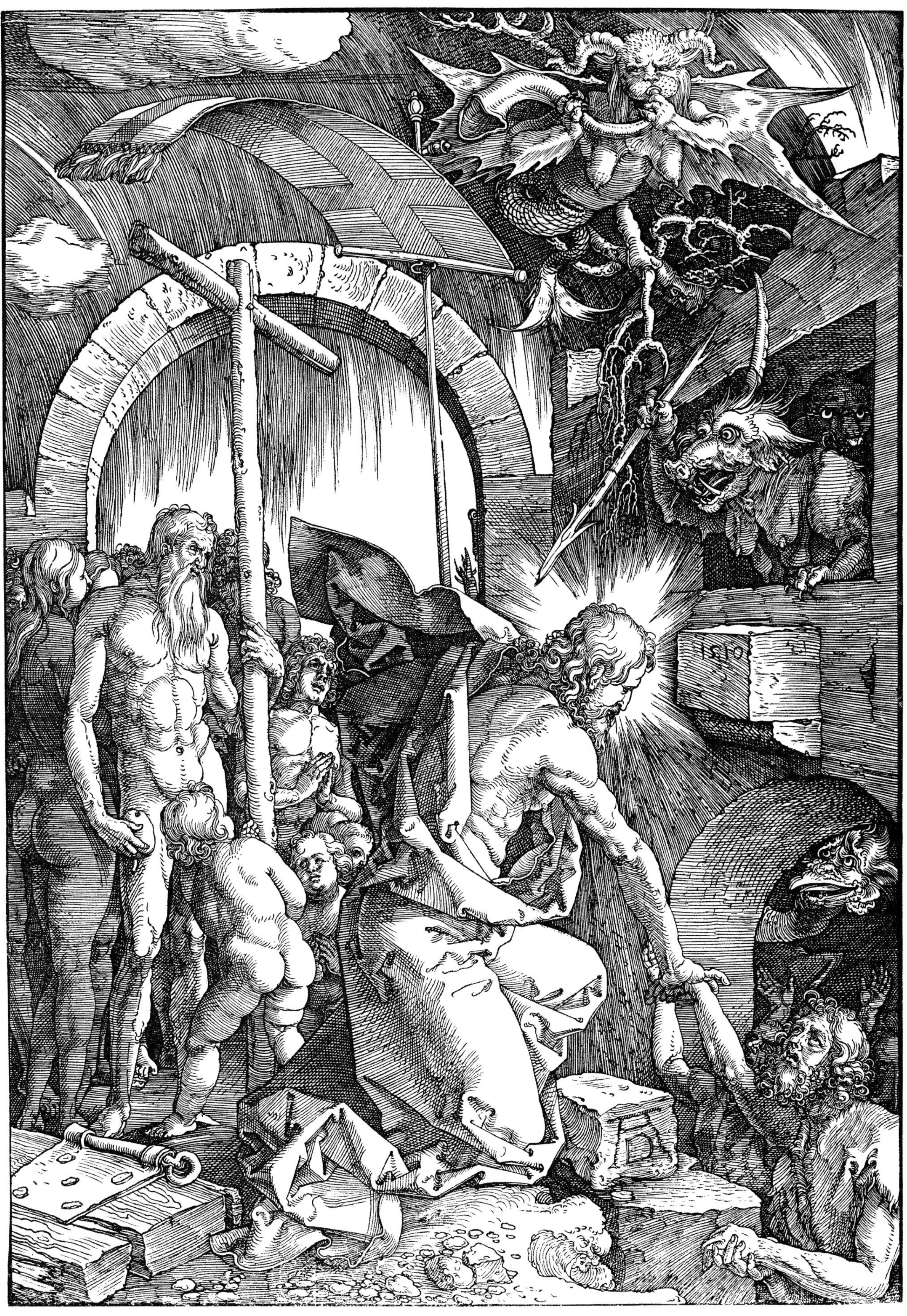

II. THE RESURRECTION

62 Now the next day, that followed the day of the preparation, the chief priests
and Pharisees came together unto Pilate,
63 Saying, Sir, we remember that that deceiver said, while he was yet alive,
After three days I will rise again.
64 Command therefore that the sepulchre be made sure until the third day,
lest his disciples come by night, and steal him away, and say unto the people,
He is risen from the dead: so the last error shall be worse than the first.
65 Pilate said unto them, Ye have a watch: go your way, make it as sure as ye can.
66 So they went, and made the sepulchre sure, sealing the stone,
and setting a watch.

1 In the end of the sabbath, as it began to dawn toward the first day of the week,
came Mary Magdalene and the other Mary to see the sepulchre.
2 And, behold, there was a great earthquake: for the angel of the Lord descended
from heaven, and came and rolled back the stone from the door, and sat upon it.
3 His countenance was like lightning, and his raiment white as snow:
4 And for fear of him the keepers did shake, and became as dead men.
5 And the angel answered and said unto the women, Fear not ye:
for I know that ye seek Jesus, which was crucified.
6 He is not here: for he is risen, as he said. Come, see the place where the Lord lay.
7 And go quickly, and tell his disciples that he is risen from the dead;
and, behold, he goeth before you into Galilee; there shall ye see him:
lo, I have told you.

MATTHEW, CHAPTER 27, VERSES 62-65, AND CHAPTER 28, VERSES 1-7

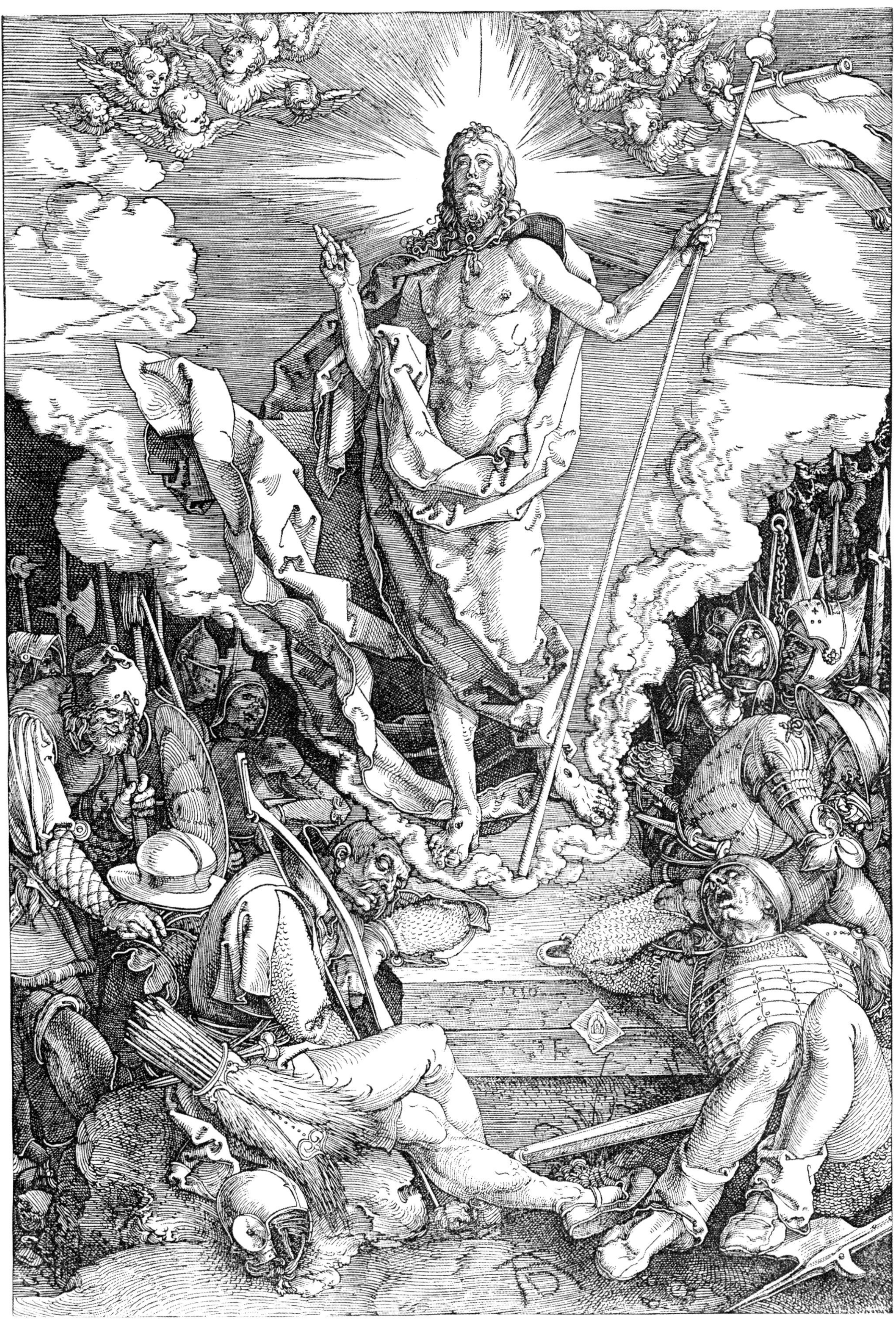

NOTE ON DÜRER'S GREAT PASSION

Dürer started work on the woodcuts of the *Great Passion* (also called the *Large Passion*, to distinguish it from the later *Small Passion*) in 1497, just before publishing the *Apocalypse with Pictures* in 1498. Work continued until 1500, by which time he had completed seven cuts. It was not until 1510 that he resumed work on the series, producing four additional cuts, the 'Last Supper', the 'Arrest of Christ', the 'Descent into Limbo' and the 'Resurrection'. By this time his style had changed considerably, so much so in fact that Vasari thought that the earlier cuts, which he considered much inferior, were produced by 'for the sake of gain, by other people who were unscrupulous enough to assign them to Albrecht'. Modern critics have acknowledged the greater sophistication of the later prints, but appreciate also the vigour and liveliness of the first seven.

In 1511 Dürer published the entire series as a book, with accompanying Latin verses in an epic style. These were composed by Benedict Schwalbe, also known as Chelidonius (c. 1460–1521), a monk and humanist writer who was abbot of the Scottish Monastery in Vienna, but was himself a native of Nuremberg like Dürer. Schwalbe also wrote elegiac verses to accompany Dürer's *Life of the Virgin*, which was published in the same year, together with a second edition of the *Apocalypse with Pictures*. All three were in the same large folio format, and Dürer referred to them as his 'three great books'. The printer was Hieronymus Höltzel (fl. 1500–1525), and each book was sold for a quarter gulden, about the price of a good pair of shoes; and they were often sold and bound together.

More woodcut art from Pallas Athene

THE APOCALYPSE WITH PICTURES
by Albrecht Dürer
16 black-and-white illustrations
ISBN 978 1 84368 213 4

In 1498, with Europe trembling before the Ottomans and mortally afraid of what the ominous year 1500 might bring, Albrecht Dürer published his *Apocalypse with Pictures*, an hallucinatory exploration of the Revelation of St John. Dürer's woodcut technique has never been equalled, and the *Apocalypse* remains one of the summits of Western art. This edition reproduces all 15 images together with their Bible texts, as well as the frontispiece Dürer added to the second edition.

SCENES FROM THE PASSION
by Lucas Cranach
16 black-and-white illustrations
ISBN 978 1 84368 258 5

The leading artist of the Reformation in Germany, and the close collaborator of Martin Luther, Lucas Cranach was one of the most influential and prolific printmakers of the northern Renaissance. His spare and eloquent images of the Passion series, begun in 1509, are among his finest creations; they have a drama and pathos that rival the work of his exact contemporary Dürer.

IN THE BEGINNING
by Edward Burne-Jones
25 black-and-white illustrations
ISBN 978 1 84368 088 8

A series of designs to illustrate the first chapters of Genesis, and intended to have been part of a Kelmscott Bible, these woodcuts were left unpublished at Burne-Jones's death and were prepared for printing by his widow Georgiana. Burne-Jones's peerless sense of design is seen at its purest in these beautiful images; and the intensely careful balance of illustration and text makes this an epitome of the Kelmscott style.

More illustration from Pallas Athene

THE FOLLIES
by Francisco de Goya
24 black-and-white illustrations
ISBN 978 1 84368 255 4

Goya's last set of etchings were made between 1815 and 1824, the dark years after the fall of Napoleon, when the artist was living in his farm, the House of the Deaf Man. Enigmatic and sinister, the etchings were not published until long after Goya's death. Variously known as 'The Proverbs', 'The Dreams', or, most often, *Los Disparates*, 'The Follies', they are some of the most compelling images in Western art and their technical virtuosity is second to none.

ELEGIES OF LOVE
by Ovid, illustrated by Auguste Rodin
31 black-and-white illustrations
ISBN 978 1 84368 163 2

These woodcut illustrations to Rodin's favourite poems, the only printed versions of Rodin's work to receive his full approval, were taken from the astonishingly free and improvisatory life drawings the sculptor made in his later years.

Privately published in 1939 in a strictly limited edition, these 31 beautiful images are very rarely seen. They are paired here with Christopher Marlowe's glittering translation, which was ceremonially burnt by the Archbishop of Canterbury in 1599.

MILLAIS'S COLLECTED ILLUSTRATIONS
by John Everett Millais
81 black-and-white illustrations
ISBN 978 1 84368 268 4

Millais, child prodigy, co-founder of the Pre-Raphaelite Brotherhood, pre-eminent portraitist of his generation, was also the leading figure in the revival of serious black-and-white work, for which English artists became renowned. This book, collected by his publisher, and republished here for the first time since 1865, shows the wide range of his work. Collected from Millais's work for Trollope, Tennyson, Collins, and the weekly periodicals over most of his long working life, these prints range from visionary romance to comedy of manners. They are some of the finest illustrations of the Victorian era.

Illustrated books by William Blake

THE GATES OF PARADISE
22 black-and-white illustrations
ISBN 978 1 84368 188 5

In this little book for children, first made in 1793, Blake charted the course of human life and experience in eighteen enigmatic emblems. Twenty-five years later, he revisited the book, adding three plates of explication and some captions. It remains one of his most accessible, yet disconcerting works.

THENOT AND COLINET
17 black-and-white illustrations
ISBN 978 1 84368 192 2

Blake's only wood engravings, made near the end of his life for a school edition of Virgil, are among his most lyrical and enduringly influential creations. This is the first time they have been published in book form, and together with the poetry that they illustrate.

Visions of little dells, and nooks, and corners of Paradise;
models of the exquisitest intense pitch of poetry
Samuel Palmer

ILLUSTRATIONS OF THE BOOK OF JOB
23 black-and-white illustrations
ISBN 978 1 84368 187 8

William Blake's last masterpiece of printmaking, commissioned by the painter John Linnell, and based on watercolours Blake had made around 1805. Three hundred copies were printed in 1826, and they earned Blake high recognition from fellow artists.

Of the highest rank in certain characters of imagination
and expression; ... in expressing conditions of glaring
and flickering light, Blake is greater than Rembrandt
John Ruskin